NATIONAL GEOGRAPHIC

D0503630

MYSTERIES OF THE MAYA

PIONEER EDITION

By Brent Goff and Kenneth Garrett

CONTENTS

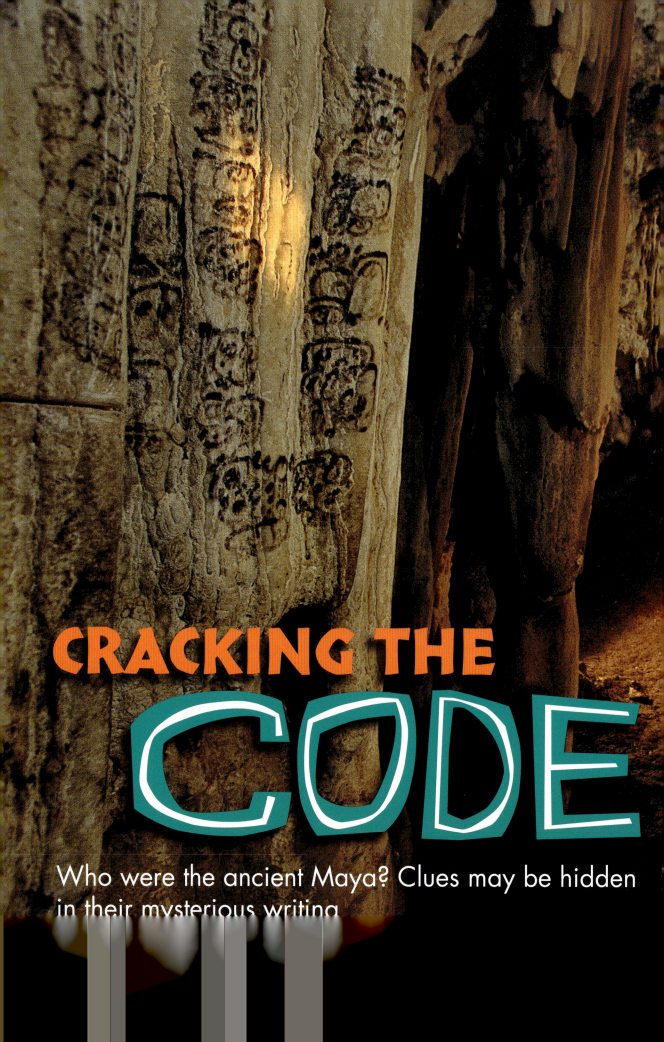

CRACKING THE
CODE

Who were the ancient Maya? Clues may be hidden in their mysterious writing.

David Stuart followed a trail deep in the rain forest. Monkeys chattered. Mosquitoes buzzed.

The 15-year-old pushed on. It was 1980. Months earlier, two farmers found something. It was a cave with wall paintings.

Now, David and his father raced to see the cave's secrets. They knew the Maya built great cities in these jungles. How did they live? Why did they leave these cities many years ago?

MAYA MYSTERY

The Stuarts reached the cave. A beam of light lit the wall. David saw **hieroglyphs**, or glyphs. Glyphs are shapes that stand for words or parts of words. He was looking at ancient Maya writing. Maybe the glyphs could help solve the Maya mysteries!

The **quest** to crack the code, or puzzle, of Maya writing began 170 years ago. In 1839, two explorers went to the jungles of Central America. They found the ruins of 44 Maya cities. They wrote a book about their journey. It made others want to know more.

DIGGING FOR CLUES

Archaeologists began searching for answers. Over time, they found many buildings. They dug up pottery and other artifacts. All were clues to how the Maya lived.

The clues tell a lot. They show that Maya cities thrived from 250 C.E. to 900 C.E. Maya cities were big. The ruins at Tikal in Guatemala include 3,000 buildings. As many as 90,000 people once lived there.

Each city was like a small country. A king ruled each one. The Maya honored the kings in their art. Pictures of the kings were painted and carved in stone.

GLYPH MYSTERY

Archaeologists also found many glyphs. Writing experts wanted to understand Maya writing. They studied the glyphs. They wondered if the Maya left a key to reading them.

In 1799, the Rosetta Stone was found in Egypt. It had Egyptian and Greek writing on it. **Scholars** could read the Greek writing. They used it to understand the Egyptian hieroglyphs. Did the Maya have some sort of Rosetta Stone, too?

Book Facts. *These pages are from a Maya book*

TIME LINE

250–900	1500s	1799
Maya civilization thrives.	The Spanish begin their conquest of Central America.	The Rosetta Stone is used to read Egyptian hieroglyphs.

EARLY LEADS

The hunt was on! Scholars looked for more clues about Maya writing. By the mid-1800s, writing experts had found three Maya books. They now had more glyphs to study.

Then, in 1862, scholars got a big break. They found an old book. It was written by Spanish priest Diego de Landa. Landa had lived with the Maya in the 1500s. In his book, Landa matched glyphs to Spanish letters. Was this the key to reading Maya glyphs?

when to plant corn and find honey.

TIME TRACKERS

Writing experts tried to use Landa's alphabet. Still, they couldn't make sense of the glyphs.

Then, in the 1880s, a scholar noticed something. The bars and dots in the glyphs followed a pattern. The pattern of bars and dots formed numbers. He realized the Maya had a counting system.

When scholars read the bars and dots, they realized that many numbers were dates. The Maya had a calendar to keep track of time!

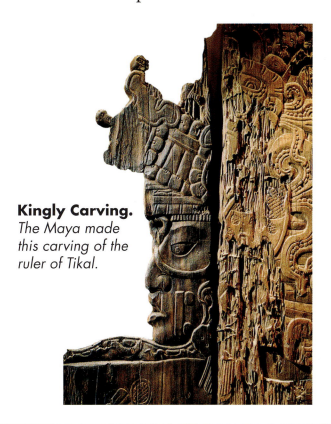

Kingly Carving. *The Maya made this carving of the ruler of Tikal.*

1839	**1862**	**1880s**	**1980**
Explorers discover Maya ruins.	A book matches some Maya glyphs to letters in the Spanish alphabet.	Scholars discover Maya numbers and calendar.	David Stuart discovers that Maya words can be written in different ways.

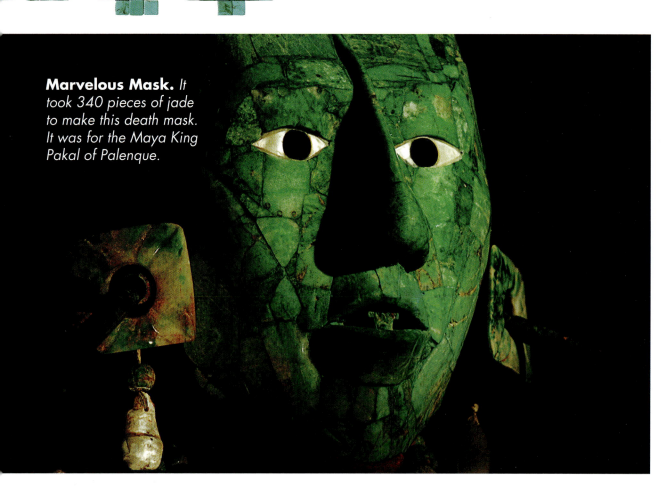

Marvelous Mask. *It took 340 pieces of jade to make this death mask. It was for the Maya King Pakal of Palenque.*

BREAKING THE CODE

By the 1950s, writing experts had identified 800 glyphs. They still couldn't read most of them. Were the meanings lost forever?

Then scholars began to see more patterns in the glyphs. Some seemed to be the names of places. Others stood for words. Many stood for sounds in the Maya language. Landa's "alphabet" began to make sense. By 1980, writing experts understood about 75 percent of the Maya glyphs.

Look for Labels. *What was this pot used for? There's a clue written on it. The top middle glyph stands for the word cacao. That means "chocolate."*

CAVE KEY

That's the year David made his trip to the cave. He stared at the cave wall. He looked at a word. He thought it was *Pax*. That's the name of a Maya month. But it looked different. He sounded it out: *Pa-xa*. It was the same word. But it was written in a different way. David had just read a Maya glyph no one had read before.

David became an expert on Maya glyphs. His work led to a new way of reading glyphs. He showed that the Maya drew different glyphs to stand for the same sounds. It's like English, where the *f* and *ph* look different but sound the same.

It took decades of hard work. Yet David and others had broken the Maya code! That means they solved the puzzle of Maya writing. Now they could learn more about the lives of the ancient Maya.

SHARING SECRETS

The glyphs fill in details of Maya history and give clues to daily life. They proved that Maya kings drank chocolate. David read a glyph on a clay pot. It said *cacao*, or "chocolate." Scientists tested another pot with the same glyph. It still had chocolate in it!

MYSTERIES REMAIN

Today, writing experts can read about 95 percent of Maya glyphs. This hasn't solved all the Maya mysteries. After 900 C.E., most Maya cities emptied. No glyphs explain what happened.

So questions remain. Yet new finds keep adding to what's known. Not long ago, David went to the ruins at San Bartolo. He saw glyphs painted on a wall. They were written between 300 B.C.E. and 200 B.C.E. It was the oldest Maya writing ever found!

What secrets do these new glyphs hold? Many can't be read yet. Code breakers have a new puzzle to solve. They will find the glyphs' meanings to make sure they are never lost again.

WORDWISE

hieroglyph: writing that uses shapes to stand for words or word parts

quest: a journey in search of something

scholar: a person who has studied something deeply

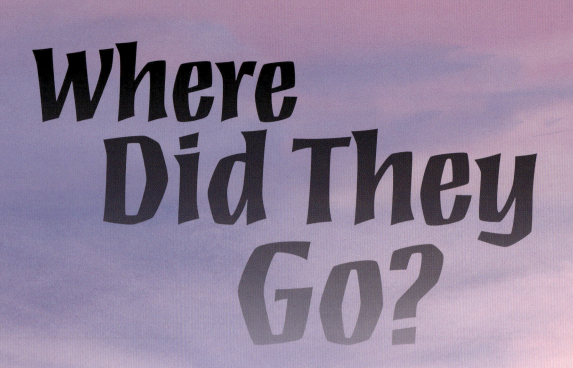

Where Did They Go?

By Kenneth Garrett
NATIONAL GEOGRAPHIC PHOTOGRAPHER

Big City. *Palenque was one of the Maya's greatest cities. The tower at the left is part of a large, stone palace.*

A lost world is hidden in Central America. Hundreds of old cities stand in the rain forests there. Once they were home to Native Americans known as the Maya.

Today those cities are empty. Pyramids and temples stand in ruins.

What happened to the Maya? Why did they leave their beautiful cities? Archaeologists have been asking these questions for years.

So have I. I take photos for National Geographic. I watch as new discoveries **reveal** answers to these questions.

On a recent assignment, I visited the ancient city of San Bartolo. Some of the earliest Maya ruins have been found there.

Peek at the Early Maya

People began building San Bartolo about 2,500 years ago. Slowly, they constructed several large stone pyramids. They hold surprises.

One pyramid has a special room. It is full of beautiful **murals**. Murals are paintings on walls.

Scientists found the murals only a few years ago. It was a huge discovery. The skill put into them was surprising. No one knew the early Maya were such good artists!

In addition, scientists found some glyphs. They are some of the oldest Maya writing ever discovered.

Clearly, San Bartolo is an important site. It isn't the only Maya place, though.

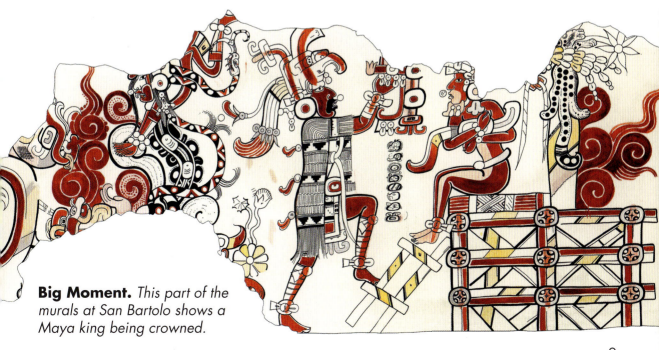

Big Moment. *This part of the murals at San Bartolo shows a Maya king being crowned.*

Cities of Stone

One of my favorite Maya places is Copán. Early on, Copán was just a small town. Perhaps 3,000 people lived there. Over time, it grew to 20,000 people. It became a great city.

Copán was small, though, next to Tikal. It was a huge city. As many as 90,000 people once lived there. Tikal is one of the most beautiful places ever.

Parts of both places still stand. They are really something. Just think about how they were built. The Maya used no wheels. They had no horses either. People did all the hard work.

Maya Life

Who lived in these great cities? Most Maya were ordinary people. They lived in houses around the cities' edges. They raised corn. That was the Maya's main food.

Some people had special skills. They were writers, potters, and more. A few people studied the sky. They watched the moon and the planets.

Then there were the rulers. Maya kings wanted people to see them as gods. So they lived in **palaces**. A Maya palace was huge. Clearly, it belonged to someone important!

Bird Man. *People used this clay vessel to burn incense. The figure is a Maya warrior wearing an eagle headdress.*

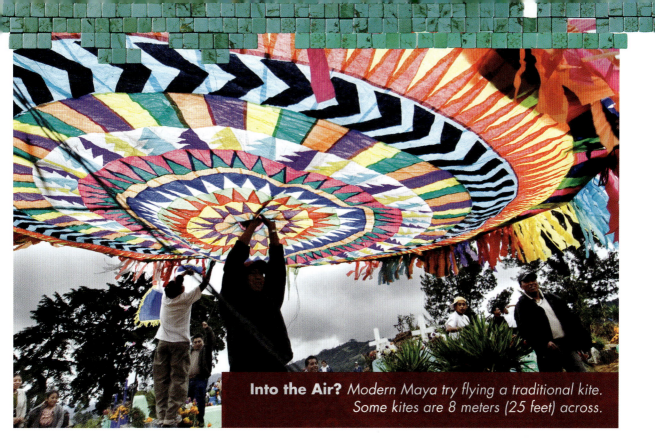

Into the Air? *Modern Maya try flying a traditional kite. Some kites are 8 meters (25 feet) across.*

Hard Times

By the year 800, the Maya had been around for hundreds of years. It seemed like life would never change. Then it did.

The great Maya cities stopped growing. People moved away. Soon, the cities lay empty.

What happened? No one knows. Perhaps it was war. Maybe it was lack of rain. Maya farming might have hurt the land.

Maya people didn't just disappear, however. North of the rain forests, new cities grew.

In the 1500s, the Spanish came. They conquered Central America. They then ruled the Maya. That meant more changes.

Great Maya Moments

The Maya live on today. People still speak Mayan languages. They follow some old customs.

People fly huge, round kites, like they did in the old days. The kites have messages for dead family members. Everyone tries to fly the kites so they reach the heavens.

Watching those kites showed me that Maya culture lives on. Taking pictures makes the moments last. I look forward to the next one!

Wordwise

mural: painting on a wall

palace: home of a king or other ruler

reveal: to make known

MANY MYSTERIES

Solve the mystery. Find the answers to these questions about the Maya.

1. Why are David Stuart's discoveries important?

2. Look at the time line. What event took place in the 1500s? How does this event help you understand Maya civilization?

3. Where did the Maya go? Explain how Kenneth Garrett answers the question.

4. How does Maya civilization compare with the civilization of ancient Egypt?

5. How have David Stuart and Kenneth Garrett helped solve the mysteries of the Maya?